A LETTER

TO THE

HON. BENJAMIN R. CURTIS,

LATE JUDGE OF THE

Supreme Court of the United States,

IN REVIEW OF HIS RECENTLY PUBLISHED PAMPHLET

ON THE

"EMANCIPATION PROCLAMATION"

OF THE PRESIDENT.

By CHARLES P. KIRKLAND,

OF NEW YORK.

NEW YORK:
LATIMER BROS. & SEYMOUR, LAW STATIONERS, 21 NASSAU ST.

1862.

To the Honorable Benjamin R. Curtis, *late Associate Justice of the Supreme Court of the United States.*

I propose, respectfully, but with perfect frankness, to review your recently published pamphlet on the subject of the President's "Emancipation Proclamation" of September 22d, 1862.

This would have been done at an earlier day, but it is only very recently that I first saw the pamphlet.

It is to be regretted that, regarding—as you profess to do—this proclamation and that of the 24th of the same month, as fraught with peril to your countrymen, you did not treat them separately. They differ radically and essentially in subject and in intent. The one is limited in its application to the rebel States, the other applies equally there and here. The one involves ultimate results and consequences of the most important and enduring character; the other is, in its very nature, temporary. The one gives rise to considerations of a kind wholly different from, and irrelevant to, the other; yet your pamphlet so confuses them together, that it is quite difficult, if not impossible, to discover what, in your view, is the distinguishing fatal error of each. Justice to the subject, which you declare to be of such momentous import; justice to the Head of this great nation, whose acts you arraign as bordering on, if not actually amounting to, the *crime* of usurpation; justice to the elevated position you so recently occupied, required that you should at least have pointed out separately, distinctly, and in the most lucid manner, the grounds on which you base a charge of such magnitude. Instead of that, we have here (to use a legal term with which you are familiar) a complete "hotch-potch." These different and distinct matters are thrown indiscriminately together; and, in many instances, no ingenuity can determine whether your argument, your illustrations, your depracatory expressions, apply to the one proclamation or to the other.

But at present I shall, so far as I can, ascertain from your pamphlet the specific complaints you make as to the "emancipation proclamation," and, if I err in attributing to you allegations as to this, which you intended solely for the other, my error will, I trust, find an apology in the mode you have adopted of treating the two subjects.

Before going further, I may be pardoned for imitating your example, and saying a word personal to myself. In some essential particulars, I stand in the same position you state yourself to occupy. I, like you, "am a member of no political party." "I withdrew," as you did, "some years ago, from all such connections." I have generally, however, exercised my privilege as one of the electoral body: and at the last presidential election I voted against the present incumbent, and at the last State senatorial election I voted for the democratic candidate in my district.

I, like you, "have no occasion to listen to the exhortations now so frequent to divest myself of party ties, and act for my country." I, too, "have nothing but my country for which to act in public affairs," and with me, too, "it is solely because I have *that* yet remaining, and know not but it may be possible to say something to my countrymen, which may aid them to form right conclusions in these dark and dangerous times that I now (through you) address them," and make the effort to aid them in "forming right conclusions" as to your views, and the subject of which you treat. Thus, my work, like yours, is purely "a work of love."

It may not be amiss to say, that there are, in fact, but two parties in our country; one that is for the country, the other that is against the country. To the former belong the vast majority of the Democratic party and the vast majority of the Republican party, and the few (alas! so few) Unionists of the South; to the latter belong the fanatical abolitionists in the Republican party, the rebel sympathisers in the Democratic party and the Rebels of the South. To the party of my country belong, I say, the great majority of both the Democratic and the Republican parties; in other words, the vast majority of the "People" of the United States—I say so, because I cannot be persuaded, that that majority, by whatever party name the individuals composing it may be called, are insensible to the blessings of the form of government under which they live, unaware, and ignorant of the indispensable importance of the preservation of the Union to their existence as a nation—forgetful, basely, ungratefully forgetful, of the heroic struggles and sacrifices of their Revolutionary fathers—deaf and dead to the earnest, paternal farewell advice and warnings of Washington, lost to all sense of patriotism, and of public virtue. And as to the millions from other lands, who are now "of us and with us," who have sought and found shelter and protection, and happiness in our Temple of Liberty, and who with such gallantry have recently fought the battles of "The United States of America," and who individually belong to the Democratic or the Republican parties, I cannot believe that these men, whether as individuals they may be called Democrats or Republicans, will ever consent to the overthrow of that Temple, or to the breaking up of those "*United* States." But notwithstanding this perfect conviction of mine, it is nevertheless, as you say, not out of place for you or for me, or for any others who choose to undertake the task, to "say something that may aid our countrymen to form right conclusions in these *dark* and dangerous" (as you call them) "times."

These words, "dark and dangerous," in the connection in which you use them, lead me to say another preliminary word before coming directly to your argument.

These words assure me, that you belong to that class of men among us, not large in number but sometimes influential in position, who, from natural temperament and disposition, or from aversion to strife of all kinds, or from a want of *proper appreciation* of the *real character* of this rebellion, (I think chiefly from the latter cause), honestly labor under a fearful distrust or a gloomy foreboding as to the result of the impending contest for the preservation of our glorious government and of our blessed Union. *I do not belong to that class of men.* I do not now believe, fear, nor apprehend, and never for a moment have believed, feared, or apprehended that a crime, such as this rebellion, a crime against the Almighty and against humanity, wholly without a parallel for enormity in the world's history and the iniquity of which can scarcely be expressed in any language known to us, I do not, I say, believe that such a crime will be permitted to be carried to a successful end, so long as "God sitteth on the throne judging right," nor until Truth shall cease to prevail over error, reason to triumph over delusion, and Right to overcome wrong.* On the contrary, I look with a clear faith and a cheerful confidence to the termination of this rebellion at no remote period, and to such a termination as will show to an admiring and approving world that this government, confessedly the most beneficent, is at the same time the most firm and enduring to be found on earth.

To proceed to the examination of your argument:

The first observation I have to make is, that throughout your paper you treat the proclamation substantially as if it were a proclamation of *absolute* emancipation in the rebel states; that is, were it *such a proclamation*, your argument would be *in substance* the same it now is.

Again, in your copy of it you entirely omit the clause in reference to *compensation;* and it will be found that a portion, and no immaterial portion, of your argument, is based on the non existence of the *conditional* and *compensatory* parts of the proclamation. It is very clear, that a proper regard to truth and fairness would have required a conspicuous place in your paper for these two distinguishing features.

With these omitted or practically concealed, you could by no possibility attain the object you profess, namely, "the aiding your countrymen in forming *right* conclusions."

A fatal error underlying your whole argument is, that in substance and effect you treat and argue this matter precisely as you would have done had there been no rebellion and *no*

---

* In speaking of the *crime* of this rebellion, the difference in a moral point of view between the *leading conspirators* and the *body of the people* of the South engaged in it should carefully be kept in view. The *former* are to be *execrated*, the latter to be *pitied ;* and while the practical effects of the wickedness of the one and of the delusions of the other, combined in action as they are, are the same, yet we are never to cease to draw the *moral distinction* just mentioned. Any one who desires to know the secret and real causes of the Rebellion, the motives and ends of the arch-conspirators, who originated it, will be gratified and instructed by a perusal of the article entitled "Slavery and Nobility, *vs.* Democracy," in the July number, 1862, of the Continental Monthly.

war; had the country been at peace; had you prepared and published your views in November, 1859, (if a similar proclamation had been then issued). You throw the veil of oblivion over the last two years; you ignore the events, that have occurred during that period and the state of things existing in the country on the 22d of September, 1862.

Though you wholly disregard it in your *argument*, yet you forcibly describe the *status* of the country on the day of its date. You say, "The war in which we are engaged is a *just and necessary* war. It *must* be prosecuted with the *whole force* of this government, till the *military power* of the South is broken and they *submit* themselves to their *duty* to obey and our *right* to have them obey the Constitution of the United States as the supreme law of the land." You thus affirm that, at the date of that proclamation, we were and now are engaged in a *war, a just and necessary war*—a war *that must be carried to a successful termination* by the exercise of the *whole force and power* of the government. You might justly have added, that it is a war infinitely worse, on the part of the rebels who caused it, than a war with any foreign nation could be, in its inception; in the mode of its conduct by the rebels; in the motives of its originators, and the ends sought to be accomplished by it. It was then by necessary consequence a war, in which all the means—and more than the means—we might legitimately resort to *in a foreign war* might and *ought* to be used and rendered available to the utmost practicable extent consistent with the rules of civilized warfare.

What, then, if we were at war with a foreign nation immediately on our borders, and that nation had within its bosom millions of slaves? Can any one, versed in the slightest degree in the principles of the law of nations and the laws of war, for a moment doubt our *right* to declare and proclaim freedom to those slaves, in case that nation did not discontinue that war within a prescribed period?

It may be asked what would be the utility, the *practicalness* of such a proclamation? I answer in your own words, "I do not propose to discuss the question whether this proclamation can have any *practical* effect on the *unhappy race* to whom it refers, nor what its *practical* consequences would be on them and on *the white population* of the United States." You discuss and I discuss simply the *constitutional right and power* of the President *under existing facts* to issue that proclamation.

We, in this discussion, are to assume that, in the contingency stated in it, it will go into actual operation as intended. Then we are to inquire what the practical effect of its thus going into actual operation would be, not on the black nor the white race, but *on the war* the rebels have declared and are carrying on. It requires but a very limited knowledge of facts to answer this inquiry. If any one fact is demonstrated with perfect clearness in this contest thus far, it is, that the slaves in the states in rebellion have furnished to those states means *indispensable* to them for carrying on and sustaining the contest on their part.*

---

* Thousands of illustations of the truth of this statement might be given. Take this one: On the second day of November, 1862, Gov. Brown, of Georgia, "Commander in Chief," issued this edict:

To the Planters of Georgia:

Since my late appeal to some of you, I am informed by Brig.-Gen. MERCER, commanding at Savannah, that but few hands have been tendered. When the impressments made by Gen. Mercer, some weeks since, were loudly complained of, it was generally said that, while the planters objected to the principle of impressments, they would promptly furnish all the labor needed, if an appeal were made to them. I am informed that Gen. Mercer now has ample authority to make impressments. If, then, a sufficient supply of labor is not tendered within ten days from this date, he will resort immediately to that means of procuring it with my full sanction, and I doubt not with the sanction of the General Assembly.

After you have been repeatedly notified of the absolute necessity for more labor to complete the fortifications adjudged by the military authorities in command to be indispensible to the defence of the key to the State, will you delay action till you are compelled to contribute means for the protection, not only of all your slaves, but of your homes, your firesides and your altars?

I will not believe that there was a want of sincerity in your professions of liberality and patriotism when many of you threatened resistance to impressment upon principle, and not because you were unwilling to aid the cause with your means.

I renew the call for negroes to complete the fortifications around Savannah, and trust that every planter in Georgia will respond by a prompt tender of one-fifth of all his working men.

As stated in my former appeal, the General in command will accept the number actually needed.

JOSEPH E BROWN.

The Governor, it will be seen, calls for "one-fifth of all the working (slaves) men." The slave population in Georgia, in 1860, exceeded 462,000; it is not an exaggerated estimate, that one in six of that population is a "working man;" this one-sixth is more than 77,000, and one-fifth of that number is upwards of 15,000. The call is therefore for 15,000 "working men," and this too in a single State, and for a limited purpose. And yet we have not the *right to try* to reader unavailable to the "enemy," this powerful force!

Without the agricultural and domestic labor of the slaves, tens of thousands of whites, who have been and now are in the rebel army, could not have been withdrawn from the cultivation of the ground, and the various other pursuits requisite to the supply, for that whole region, of the actual necessaries of life. Without the slaves, their numerous and extensive earthworks, fortifications, and the like, their immense transportation of military stores and munitions, a vast amount of labor in camps and on marches (to say nothing of the actual service as *soldiers*, said in many instances to have been rendered by slaves), could by no possibility have been accomplished.

The intent and design of the proclamation, its actual effect, if it has its *intended* operation, is to forever deprive the "enemy" of this vital, absolutely essential, and, as I have just said, *indispensable*, means of carrying on *the war*. In reason, in common sense, in national law, in the law of civilized war, what objection can exist to our using our power to attain an end so just, so lawful, and I may say so beneficent, and so humane, as thus depriving our "enemy" of his means of warfare? I do not believe that you, on more mature reflection, will deny the truth of what I have just stated.

But you say, "grant that we have this power and this right, they cannot be exercised *by the President*," and for the exercise of this power, he is charged by you with "usurpation."

A few considerations will show the fallacy, the manifest unsoundness and error of your views and arguments on this point I may, in the first place, remark that the very *title* of your pamphlet, "*Executive Power*," is a "delusion and a snare." The case does not give rise to the investigation of the President's "executive power." The word "executive," manifestly and from the whole context of the Constitution, has reference to the *civil* power of the President, to his various civil duties as the head of the nation, in "seeing that the laws are executed"—to his duties in time of *peace*, though of course the same "executive" duties still continue in time of war; but to them, *in that event*, are superadded others, which, in no just or proper sense, can be termed "executive," but which pertain to him *in time of war* as "Commander-in-Chief. These latter duties are provided for by the letter and by the spirit of other provisions of the Constitution, by the very nature and necessity of the case, by the first law of nature and of nations, the *law of self-preservation.* What is the meaning and intent of the constitutional direction to the President, "that he shall *preserve, protect, and defend the Constitution,*" unless in *time of war* he can do so in his capacity of "Commander-in-Chief," unless in *time of war*, he shall have the power to adopt and carry out *as to the enemy* such measures as the *laws of war* justify, and as he may deem necessary. Is the Constitution designed to *do away* these laws, and render them inapplicable to our nation—in other words, is the Constitution a *felo de se?* It cannot be denied, that in time of war, at least, the President, while in a civil sense the "executive" is at the same time the military head of the nation—"the Commander-in-Chief"—and as such *his* "command" is necessarily co-extensive with the country.

I cannot, on this point, quote anything more true and more apposite than a paragraph of your own. "*In time of war, without any special legislation, the* (our) *Commander-in-Chief is lawfully empowered by the Constitution and laws of the United States to do whatever is necessary and is sanctioned by the laws of war to accomplish the lawful objects of his command.*"

This is, undoubtedly, the constitutional law of the land, and being so, it of necessity upsets and overturns all your objections to the proclamation in question. The "lawful object" of the President at this moment is to preserve the Constitution by putting an end to this rebellion. In order to do this, it is necessary to deprive the rebels of their means of sustaining the rebellion—one of the most effective and available of those means, as just shown, is their slaves; the intent and object of the proclamation are to deprive them of those means. The so depriving them "is sanctioned by the laws of war," and, consequently, this act of the President is, within your own doctrine, perfectly legal and constitutional.

The same argument which you make against presidential power was made in Cross v. Harrison, 16 Howard, 164, in the Supreme Court of the United States, in a case occurring during, and arising out of, our war with Mexico, in the judgment in which case you, as one of the Justices of that Court, concurred.

In that case the President, without any specific provision in the Constitution—without any law of Congress pre-existing or adopted for the occasion, created a civil government in California, established a war tariff, and (by his agents) collected duties. The Court held that these acts (to use their own language) "were rightful and constitutional, though Congress had passed no law on the subject;" that "those acts of the President were the exercise of a *belligerent right*; that they were according to the *law of arms* and right on the *general principles of war* and peace." Who will allege, that the acts of the President on that occasion were not, to say the least, as unauthorized by the Constitution and the law as his proclamation in the present case? And yet you did not dissent from the judgment of the Court, you did not speak of those acts as acts of "Executive" power, for the term would have been there, as it is here, wholly inapplicable; you did not then charge the President with usurpation. The whole case there was, as it is here, a case arising out of *belligerent* rights and duties, out of a *state of war;* and the President's acts were there, as here, not in contradiction to, and disparagement of, the Constitution, but consistent therewith, on the great ground that the Constitution nowhere repeals, but, on the contrary, from the necessities of its own existence and preservation, recognizes the *laws of war* in a *state of war.* Similar authorities in abundance might be cited, but it would be a work of supererogation.

It may not be amiss, however, to refer in this connection to the honored name of John Quincy Adams, on the *very* point now in question, namely, the constitutional right of the President to issue *this* proclamation.

No citizen of this land will deny to Mr. Adams as perfect an acquaintance with the spirit and nature of our institutions, as minute a knowledge of the provisions, expressed and implied, of the constitution, and as ardent a desire to preserve them in their purity, as were ever possessed by any man living or dead. He was distinguished, too, for the most delicate moral sense, the purest integrity, and the deepest conscientiousness. I think no man who has taken an official oath ever felt a more earnest and constant desire on no occasion to violate it. Now, Mr. Adams, while a member of the House of Representatives, in a debate in the House, on an important subject, in April, 1842, after stating that slavery was abolished in Columbia, first by the Spanish *General* Murillo, and secondly by the American *General* Bolivar, by virtue of a *military command* given at *the head of the army*, and that its abolition continued to this day, declares that "in a state of *actual war* the *laws of war* take precedence over civil laws and municipal institutions. I lay this down as the law of nations. I say that the military authority takes for the time the place of all municipal institutions, slavery among the rest, and that under *that* state of things, so far from its being true that the States, where slavery exists, have the exclusive management of the subject, not only the President of the United States, but the (subordinate) commander of the army has *the power to order the emancipation of the slaves*." This is the "true saying" of a great constitutional lawyer, a pure patriot, a conscientious man—Indeed, I doubt whether any man in this country, whose position entitles his opinions to any consideration, will be found to concur in your views. They are not adopted—indeed, they are repudiated by the most prominent leader of the Democratic party. Thus, Mr. John Van Buren (in a speech before the Democratic Union Association of the city of New York, on the 10th of November, instant) said: "I never said anything in reference to that proclamation except that it was a matter of questionable expediency. I have *never* deemed it *unconstitutional*. I have never even asserted that, as a *war measure* it might not have been expedient." It would seem idle to add more in demonstration of the clear, unquestionable *power* of the President (I may say, of his solemn *duty*) "as commander in chief," in the exercise of a military power, "during a state of war," to issue the proclamation in question.

The ground of objection you most prominently put forth is, indeed, extraordinary, and, without offence I trust I may say, monstrous. It is no more nor less than this: "The persons who are the subjects of this proclamation are held to service by the *laws of the States* in which they reside, enacted by State authority." "This proclamation by an executive decree proposes to *repeal and annul valid State laws*, which regulate the domestic relations of their people," and this "as a punishment against the entire people of a State by reason of the criminal conduct of a *governing majority* of its people." Never was more error, gross, palpable, grievous, found in a single brief paragraph. Mark the existing state of things. These "States" are each and every of them in rebellion against their country and their Government; they are waging against it the most bloody and relentless war; they totally condemn and repudiate the constitution of their country; they deny that it has any, the least, authority over them; they are making almost superhuman efforts to overthrow and destroy it; the people, as individuals, and the States in their corporate, municipal capacities go hand in hand together in this awful work, and yet you claim for them the *protection* of that very constitution; you claim the inviolability of their *State* laws under *that constitution*. You claim that those *laws* are "valid" and operative, and are to shield and protect, aid and assist them in their unhallowed attempt to destroy their country!! It is difficult to imagine under what hallucination you were laboring when you gave utterance to those sentiments. The bare statement of the case must carry to every sane mind, North and South, the instant refutation of your propositions. The very rebels themselves, to whom you offer the protection of the "constitution," would, with wrathful indignation, spurn the offer.

You speak of the proclamation as a "threatened penalty"— as "a punishment to the entire people of a state .... by reason of the criminal conduct of a governing majority of the people."

I have already shown, satisfactorily I trust, that the act of the President partakes in no sense of the character of a "penalty" or "a punishment," but is simply the exercise of his constitutional power, in a time of war, to devise and adopt and carry out against the enemy such measures as he may judge to be for the good of his country; for the defeat of that enemy, and for the successful and speedy ending of "the war." You draw a distinction, unheard of, I imagine, till announced by you, a distinction between the "people of a State," and the "governing majority" of that people; a distinction, too, which is to operate, *in a time war*, *against* the party with whom that "State" is at war!! I venture to say, that no writer on the law of nations, no judicial tribunal, no intelligent man, has up to this hour, believed or stated that, in the case of foreign war above supposed, the "governing majority" was not to all legal and all practical purposes, "the State." Were the United States at war with any foreign power—a war sanctioned by the "governing majority," (as our war of 1812,) but a war which you and others (a minority) wholly disapproved; and that foreign power adopted some war measure which would operate on "the entire people," of the United States, could you and your associates of the minority, or any principle of law, military or civil, of justice, of reason, or of mercy, claim exemption from the effects of that measure? The case supposed is precisely the case as it now exists between the "United States of America" on the one hand, and the "Rebel States and people," on the other.

Again, you state as a serious, if not conclusive objection to the proclamation, that "it is on the slaves of loyal persons or of those who from their *tender years*, or other disability, cannot be either disloyal or otherwise, that the proclamation is to operate." Have your countrymen at this hour, to learn for the first time, that the "sun shines alike on the just and on the unjust," that storms and whirlwind overwhelm at the same time the righteous and the wicked and that the calamities of war, from the very necessity of the case, fall indiscriminately on the innocent and the guilty, the strong and the helpless, on those of mature and those of "tender years?" But as to this last objection, it lacks one material quality, namely, foundation in fact. That part of the proclamation, which you have so strangely, as observed above, omitted, provides for the case of the very persons for whom your sympathies are excited. It pledges to them compensation. I say "pledges," for it declares "that the Executive will in due time recommend that all persons who have remained loyal, (of course including in its spirit those who from tender years, or otherwise were incapable of being disloyal,) shall be *compensated* for all losses by acts of the United States, including *the loss of slaves.*" No future Congress of the United States will be so lost to all sense of honor and obligation as not to pass, and no future President so degraded as not to approve, a bill redeeming this solemn and sacred "pledge" of the Head of the nation.

Again, you advert in no part of your argument, to the vital fact that this proclamation is not absolute and unconditional, but that it depends even for its existence *practically* on the acts and will of the rebels themselves. If they so elect, *it is never to go into operation*, and they have abundant time to make that election, namely, from the 22d of September, 1862, to the 1st day of January, 1863. But your argument, *in all its essential particulars*, would have been just the same as you now address it to your fellow-citizens, if this proclamation had been absolute, had declared universal emancipation, to go into effect on the day of its date, and (as already remarked) had not provided compensation to the loyal, and had been issued in a time of profound peace.

You profess, in your argument, simply to examine "the nature and extent, and the asserted source of the power by which it is claimed that the issuing of this proclamation was authorized;" and it was "for the purpose of saying something to your countrymen to aid them in forming *right conclusions*," that you "reluctantly addressed them." The policy, the expediency, the utility, the practical effects, *per se*, of the proclamation, you say, you do not "propose to discuss," yet you *intimate*, that by means of this proclamation, if executed, "scenes of bloodshed and worse than bloodshed are to be passed through," and you express, in no unequivocal manner, a doubt "as to the lawfulness, in any Christian or civilized land, of the use of such means (that is, this proclamation) to attain any end." You intimate, too, that "a servile war is to be invoked to help twenty millions of the white race to assert the rightful authority of the Constitution and laws of their country." All these direful forebodings are put forth in half a dozen lines, certainly not to "aid your fellow citizens in forming right conclusions," but through their sympathies and their fears to induce the concurrence of their reason in your views as to the *power* to do the act in question. These "givings out" of yours require a passing notice.

In the first place, where is your authority for the allegations as to "scenes of bloodshed and a servile war?" I am not an abolitionist, nor a believer in the *social and political* equality of the black and white races (though I have an opinion on the subject of the effect of the *institution* of slavery on the white man and white woman, who have been nurtured under its influence, and on the question of the compatability of the institution with a republican form of government). I am even called by some a pro-slavery man. Yet I see no "scenes of bloodshed," no "servile war," in the event of the practical carrying out of this proclamation. This, however, is a mere matter of speculation and opinion, and while I freely concede your right to entertain your own, I claim my right to entertain mine. Our means of forming our opinions are the same; we both have the same lights, and the result alone can show which of us is right.

But, in the next place, assuming the consequences to be *just such* as you imagine, who is responsible for those consequences? They cannot come, as you will admit, if the rebels *return to their allegiance;* if they cease their unhallowed efforts to overthrow their government; if they become dutiful citizens. If they do not, it is not your fault nor mine, nor that of our fellow-citizens, nor of the President, nor of the government of the United States—it is solely, wholly, unquestionably, *their own.*

Again, you look with evident heartfelt horror at the events which you thus contemplate. Have you no horror, no tears of sympathy, no "bowels of compassion," when you reflect on the multitudes, the thousands of valuable loyal lives lost, homes grief-stricken, parents rendered childless, and children rendered orphans; the desolation and misery of whole neighborhoods, to say nothing of the enormous material destruction caused to citizens of the loyal states in this war—a war on our part, as you say, "so just and necessary," and on the part of the rebels so wicked, so wanton, so utterly causeless, and so wholly unjustifiable. Though no man of humanity could look with other than deep distress on the "scenes of bloodshed," and the "servile war," you imagine (should they become realities), surely it cannot be believed, that the amount of distress and suffering, that would thus ensue, would equal—it surely cannot surpass—the distress and suffering that have already been endured by the loyal citizens of this republic in consequence of this rebellion.

You doubt the "lawfulness," in this Christian and civilized land, of the use of such means (as this proclamation) to attain *any* end. And has it come to this, that a distinguished citizen of the republic doubts, whether a proclamation emancipating the slaves in those States, which shall be in rebellion on the first of January next, may not be "used as the means" "to attain the end" (granting that it may *thereby* be attained) of ending this war of rebellion, and thus of saving our Constitution, our government, our Union, and of still preserving for ourselves and for coming generations, here and elsewhere, the only real Temple of civil and religious liberty in which men can worship on earth. You speak of "lawfulness" in this connection rather in a *moral* than in any other sense; the right and power in *a legal and constitutional sense*, to issue this proclamation has already been demonstrated.

In a document intended, "after study and reflection," "to aid the citizens of this republic to form a right conclusion" on matters of surpassing magnitude and solemnity—matters imperilling their very liberties, as you state, a religious, scrupulous regard to truth in every material respect, was, of course, to be expected; and departure from truth may consist as well in omission and suppression as in direct assertion. I have already mentioned that you have wholly omitted, in the statement of the proclamation, the compensatory part, and that you omit to bring forward, except merely incidentally, another most material part of it, namely, its conditional, *alternative* character.

Whether your statement as to the "social condition of nine millions of men," has reference to both white and black, or to the white only, it is difficult to determine from the context; if it has reference to the white, you commit a very serious error; for the whole white population of the rebel states (to which alone the proclamation and your argument relate), according to the last census (1860), does not exceed four and one half millions.

In quoting the opinion of the lamented Judge Woodbury, you omit to state that it was a *dissenting* opinion, concurred in by no other Judge, founded essentially, if not solely, on the fact assumed by him, that at the time, in question in that case, "a state of war " *did not* exist in Rhode Island, where the matter arose. In so grave a paper prepared, as you assert, so deliberately, put forth under an imperative and resistless impulse of patriotic apprehension that the liberties of the country were in imminent peril, (not from the rebellion, but from the acts of the President, designed to crush the rebellion), in such a paper, I say, it would seem that we ought not to be terrified by "portentous clouds," "gigantic shadows," the phrase "usurpation of power," often repeated, the "loss of his head by Charles I." "seven hundred years of struggles against arbitrary power," and many other similar appeals, *by modes of expression*, to anything but that *calm reason*, which enables us to "form right conclusions in dark and dangerous times." Much less in *such* a grave document from such a source, should important stress be laid on the expression, of an unnamed and irresponsible editor of a newspaper, "that nobody pretends that this act is constitutional, and nobody cares whether it is or not." That this editor was at least a very inferior constitutional lawyer, is very clear, and that this text from his paper should have furnished a peg, on which to hang an alarming commentary on the "lawlessness" of the times, is at least extraordinary, and that lawlessness too, *not* the lawlessness of *rebels* nor of *rebel sympathizers.*

You ask, in view of the President's proclamation, "Who can imagine what is to come out of this great and desperate struggle? The military power of eleven of these states being destroyed, what then? What is to be their condition? What is to be our condition?"

Your questions admit of a ready answer. *The United States of America* are to come out of the struggle, a great, a united, a powerful, a free people, purified by the fires of adversity, and taught by their tremendous calamities the lessons of moderation and humility. The *people of the rebel states*, who choose to remain in them, are to come out of the struggle as citizens of states forming a part, as heretofore, *of the United States*, and with them, and as parts of them, they are in future to enjoy the blessings of a well regulated liberty, they having, in the mean time been taught a lesson of infinitely greater severity than that by which their brethren of the loyal states have been instructed. Whatever they have necessarily and legitimately lost in material things, by reason of *the war* they have waged, is, of course, lost to them forever; if their slave property is thus lost, *it is lost*, and that is all that can be said as to that. Then "their condition" and "our condition" is to be *in substance* just what it was before the rebellion, and what it would have continued to be but for the rebellion, with this only difference, that they and we will have learned the priceless value of the Union, and for generations to come treason and rebellion will not raise their horrid heads.

Perhaps you may call this the dream of an enthusiast. Rely on it, I speak only the words of "truth and soberness;" and if you are spared for a brief period, you will be rejoiced, I trust, to witness their full realization. *Rejoiced*, I say, because from your pamphlet, you would have your countrymen infer, and I am bound to presume, that nothing but your intense love of your and their country and your agitating apprehensions that the "principles of liberty" are greviously to suffer (not from *the rebellion*, but from the acts of *the President*), has induced you to address them.

You say the "cry of disloyalty" has been raised against any one who should question these executive acts. I know not whether that epithet has been applied to you; if it has been, I am bound to believe that the imputation was without cause, and that you are a faithful, loyal citizen of the Republic. But the greatest and the best are liable to err, and I may be permitted to say, that, however honestly and sincerely you entertain the sentiments you express, you have selected an inopportune moment for their expression; and that at this particular period of our country's history, your "studies and reflections," your time and your efforts, would, to say the least, have been more benignly and gracefully employed in presenting to your countrymen a life-like picture of the *real* character of this rebellion, and in impressing on them with stirring and glowing eloquence the momentous duty it devolved on them. You could, with perfect verity, have told them, that this war, inaugurated by the rebel States, was wholly and absolutely *without cause:* in proof

of that assertion, you could have stated three facts, so undeniable that the hardiest rebel, not bereft of reason, would not dispute them.

First.—That on the 1st day of November, 1860, no people on the globe were in the more perfect enjoyment of civil and religious liberty, of social, personal, and domestic security; of more entire protection in the possession and use of all their property, of *every kind;* and of more material prosperity, than the people of the eleven rebel States.

Second.—That for all these blessings, as great as were ever vouchsafed by God to man, those people were indebted entirely to that Constitution and that Union which their rebellion was undertaken to destroy.

Third.—That from the day of the organization of the Government under that Constitution, in the year 1789, down to the day when this rebellion began its infamous and unhallowed work, there never had been, on the part of that Government, a single act of hostility, nor even of unkindness, toward these States or their people.

You should then have pointed out to your "countrymen," in language more persuasive and emphatic than I can use, their solemn and imperative duty as patriots, as christians, and as men, in this hour of their country's suffering and peril; and you should have told them that if these times are, as you say, "dark and dangerous," this darkness and this danger have been caused by the wicked acts of these rebellious men. In such an address to your countrymen, your dedication would have been not merely "To all persons who have sworn to support the Constitution of the United States, and to all citizens who value the principles of civil liberty which that Constitution embodies, and for the preservation of which it is our only security," but also, "to all persons who abhor treason and rebellion against that Constitution, and to all who prize the inestimable blessings of our hallowed Union, and to all who hold dear the farewell words of the Father of his country."

I had intended, in this letter, to comment on that part of your pamphlet which relates to the President's proclamation of the 24th of September, 1862, but this paper is already sufficiently extended. It would, I think, be easy to show that the dreadful dangers you apprehend are, in truth, to use your own terms, "portentous clouds" and "gigantic shadows" of your own creation. At any rate you may rest assured, if you and I and all others of our fellow citizens, outside of the rebel states, shall make honest, earnest, determined efforts for the putting an effective end to this rebellion (and that such will be the case I, loving my country and knowing the *unspeakable value of the stake*, have no right nor reason to doubt), those efforts will be crowned with speedy and triumphant success, peace and harmony will be restored to the republic, the "principles of civil liberty" will not have suffered, and the bugbears of "usurpation," "arbitrary power," and other similar chimeras, which excited imaginations and gloomy tempers have evoked, will disappear forever.

Had you been an unknown and obscure citizen, any notice of your pamphlet would have been supererogatory; but because of the influence calculated to be exerted by anything coming from the pen of one who had but recently been the incumbent of the highest office in the gift of the Government, and who is now in the exalted walks of social and professional life, I have deemed it my duty to present these views of your argument, and thus "possibly to aid my countrymen" in "forming right conclusions" as to its merits and the merits of the subject of which it treats.

I hear that others have published answers to your paper. Not having seen any of them, I know not but that I may have merely repeated their views; if so, no harm is done; if I have presented any that are new, "possibly" some good may result.

New York, Nov. 28th, 1862.

CHARLES P. KIRKLAND.

www.ingramcontent.com/pod-product-compliance
Lightning Source LLC
LaVergne TN
LVHW020634110826
845149LV00004B/1186
9781418191450